ASHBURNHAM INSIGHTS

Intercession

A re-reading of Scripture by

Timothy Pain

KINGSWAY PUBLICATIONS

EASTBOURNE

ISBN 0 86065 483 4

Unless otherwise indicated biblical quotations are from
the Jerusalem Bible, copyright © Darton, Longman & Todd Ltd
and Doubleday & Co. Inc. 1966, 1967, 1968

*Cover photo shows front water
and the main bridge at Ashburnham Place
(colour photograph by Judges Postcards Ltd, Hastings).*

Printed in Great Britain for
KINGSWAY PUBLICATIONS LTD
Lottbridge Drove, Eastbourne, E. Sussex BN23 6NT by
Richard Clay (The Chaucer Press) Ltd, Bungay, Suffolk
Typeset by Nuprint Services Ltd, Harpenden, Herts AL5 4SE

INTERCESSION

Contents

Foreword to the Series

I am very pleased to commend this series of *Ashburnham Insights* which have come from the pen of Timothy Pain. Those of us who have watched developments at Ashburnham Place over the last few years have been particularly intrigued with the way things have developed. The careful thinking in these volumes comes from a background of faithful believing prayer for many years, and a deep concern for renewal and revival.

When there is an emphasis on experience, and when the subjective element in Christian living is to the fore, there is more need than ever for scriptural foundations. That is why we should be grateful to Tim for the obvious care he has taken to 'test everything', while at the same time to obey the apostolic injunction to 'despise not prophesyings'. Both should play their part in balanced Christian living.

Tim is not afraid to break new ground, and his *Insights* on speaking in tongues will be challenging to those of us who need it. I like the living way he writes, and I am sure these small books will have the wide readership they deserve.

Canon Michael Harper

This series of short books is dedicated to the memory of my father, A. F. Pain (1915-1982).

He emerged from the Deptford slums, without education or refinement, as a natural leader of men. He was radical and traditional, patient and impetuous, obstinate and flexible, gentle and ruthless; loved or loathed by all he met. He faithfully served Christ, the church, his family and the people of Brixton.

Introduction

This series has been inspired by members of the Ash-burnham Stable Family. This is a Christian community, part resident at Ashburnham Place (a Christian training centre) and part scattered throughout the villages and small towns of East Sussex. It is our calling to maintain an un-broken 'Chain of Prayer' within the Palladian Stable which is adjacent to Ashburnham Place. We pray, by day and night, for the renewal and spiritual unity of all Christian churches in East Sussex. It is our conviction that the hope of the world lies in the renewal of the church, and as one expression of this we have taken it upon ourselves to share in a serious re-reading of Holy Scripture.

It seems to me that much contemporary teaching is based on experience rather than the Bible. Just as the members of the Stable Family have gained courage to move away from the shallow waters of their varied experiences and tradi-tions, so we urge you to let go and swim with Jesus in the raging torrent of living waters which is eternal life in the Spirit.

This book is humbly offered to the church as my personal re-reading with regard to intercession. It has been lived in, worked out and written down in community. It is the product of much study and prayer; reading and listening;

experimentation and embarrassment; banter and disagreement. Some within the Stable Family still lovingly dissent from a few of my conclusions! Much of the material was originally worked on by the Rev. Edmund Heddle and myself for our conference weekends, when groups take time apart to be with God.

In recent years God has called the Stable Family to new depths of prayer and warfare. These I humbly share. They are not the last words on intercession. Those can never be written. What follows is simply a statement of where God has led this community—thus far. It is our fervent hope and prayer that God will lead us 'farther up and farther in', so that this book becomes an embarrassment to us because of its shallowness and inevitable errors.

These *Ashburnham Insights* have been written with housegroup leaders in mind. One of the great works of the Spirit in the last fifteen years has been the emergence and establishment of house groups. It is my prayer that these four books will aid these leaders in their high and holy calling.

I have tried to write in a way that is simple enough to satisfy the sincere seeker, but is sufficiently thorough to persuade those called to teach and lead in the church. The scripture references should all be looked up and examined as you proceed through the text. Bible quotations are normally taken from the Jerusalem Bible.

Any plaudits should be shared between John and Marlis Bickersteth, Helen Brown, Winifred Cox, Edmund Heddle, Gay Hyde, Jo and Susie Marriott, Margery May, Dennis and Pat Nolan, Alan Pain, Barbara Stidwill, Muriel Teideman, Roger and Penny Willcock and my wife Alison. Their prayers, patience, comments, advice, encouragement, work and love have brought the Insights from gestation to publication.

Timothy Pain

The renewal lives by the re-reading of the New Testament.

Cardinal Suenens

Back to the Bible or back to the jungle.

Luis Palau

...Doubt wisely; in strange way
To stand inquiring right is not to stray;
To sleep or run wrong is.

John Donne

Implore his aid, in his decision rest,
Secure whate'er he gives, he gives the best.

Samuel Johnson

When God intends great mercy for His people, the first thing He does is set them a praying.

Matthew Henry

Passionate, pleading, persistent prayer is always the prelude to revival.

William Sangster

Intercession

One evangelical phrase upon which I, and countless others, were raised was, 'the prayer-meeting is the powerhouse of the church'. This still remains today as a popular, widely believed and wholly inaccurate cliché. Any young blood who wants to enlist the support of aged clerics has only to shake his head sagely and mutter sadly about the dearth of prayer-meetings in these days; sympathetic heads will soon be nodding. In 1975 most evangelical churches still organized a weekly intercessory prayer-meeting. By 1985 most such meetings had closed. This, together with the mysterious disappearance of the 'long prayer' and a less legalistic attitude to daily 'quiet times', has led many to wonder when choruses will have completely replaced intercession in the Christian experience.

The cliché was inaccurate because prayer, not prayer-meetings, is the powerhouse of a church. Post Harringay (1954) prayer-meetings were full of sincerity, but empty of fire. They were stale, poorly supported and a pale caricature of the glorious reality described by Charles Finney in *Meetings for Prayer*[1] which had spawned their ancestors. The intercessory prayers were extemporary, but repeated at regular intervals. There was little expectation of fulfilment, indeed the intercessions were usually so vague as to

13

preclude fulfilment. And so the Holy Spirit closed down tens of thousands of such meetings. They had served God's purpose well in their own generation.

The prayer-meeting was only a 'wineskin' to contain the precious wine of intercessory prayer. Throughout history there have been many other wineskins—'Aaron and Hur Societies' and 'Prayers Progress' in the early nineteenth century; the mass prayer gatherings of the late nineteenth century; the Moravian Chain of Prayer in the eighteenth century; the seven times daily prayer of monasticism. In fact, twelfth century monasticism provides us with an interesting historical parallel to the contemporary charismatic scene.

By A.D. 1100 Benedictine monasteries had spread along the lucrative pilgrim routes and become enormously wealthy. The monks were spending less and less time in work and prayer, and more and more of each day worshipping in the language of plainsong—from which they derived enormous personal pleasure. In five hundred years the ideals and reforms of St Benedict had spread everywhere, and had everywhere been compromised. Into this cosy world of worship and wealth strode St Bernard of Clairvaux with his message: 'Arouse yourself, gird your loins, put aside idleness, grasp the nettle and do some hard work.' In the following forty years, 342 monasteries were 'planted', not on the comfortable pilgrim routes, but in the wild unevangelized parts of Europe. Through St Bernard, intercession and evangelism returned to the twelfth century monastic orders.

In the last few years, evangelism has returned to the charismatic agenda. God has used many agents, but the three most obvious are the disappointments of Mission England; the startling house-church discovery of the word 'evangelist' in Ephesians 4:11; and the delightful influence of John Wimber's training conferences. Now intercession needs to experience a similar renaissance. Throughout history, intercession and evangelism have been inseparable. Intercession without evangelism is a foundation without a house, and evangelism without intercession is a house with no foundation. Alternative wineskins to 'prayer-meetings' need to be established to encourage and establish intercession in renewed churches. The time has come for churches to remember that intercessory prayer is the powerhouse of a church. This little book is written with the prayer that the principles of scriptural intercession, and their association with biblical evangelism, will be relearnt and applied in the churches of those who read it.

What Is Intercession?

The common understanding of intercession is straightfor-
ward and simple: it is prayer to God for others. William
Law defined it in *A serious call to a devout and holy life* as 'a
praying to God and interceding with Him for our fellow-
creatures'.[2] Andrew Murray described it in his introduction
to *The Ministry of Intercession* as 'asking and receiving
heavenly gifts to carry to men'.[3] This may suggest that
intercession is like any other prayer, the only difference
being that instead of thanksgiving or prayer for oneself, it is
prayer for others—with 'others' as the distinguishing
feature. Little mention is made of the 'praying' as differing
from other forms of prayer. But to restrict a description of
intercession to 'prayer for others' is to dilute its strength.
Intercession is strong prayer. I would define it as 'a divinely-
appointed face to face struggle with God that is survived;
the survivor then persistently pleading with God either for
or against another'.

Exodus 33:11–34:30 is an outstanding example of biblical
intercession and merits careful reading. It contains most of
the elements which will be expanded throughout this book.
Moses was involved in a face to face confrontation with
God on behalf of others. He pleaded for the glory of God to
be seen and was then given a task to perform. He had to

Crofton Park Baptist Church, London

In 1966 the Holy Spirit began moving in a new way in this inner city church. Gordon Campbell, the new minister, introduced a much greater emphasis on prayer and so the congregation soon dropped in numbers.

During 1967, three monthly house prayer groups were started to supplement the weekly church prayer meeting. On January 6th 1969, the first half-night of prayer took place. From then until 1974 nine such 'half-nights' were held and these were all times of real power and influence. Within two years eighty out of an average Sunday congregation of a hundred were attending these half-nights of prayer. Many of these had never been to a prayer meeting before and the weekly prayer meeting quickly increased to over fifty attenders.

Praise, worship, intercession and prayer for guidance were all part of those evenings. The spiritual life of the church deepened and the sense of fellowship and love between members grew. During this period many people were converted, some of whom are now in full-time service and the congregation began to increase in size.

The church's first 'day of fasting' was on January 6th 1974, followed immediately by another half-night of prayer. Resulting from this, two people heard and obeyed God's call to train at a Bible College.

At the close of Gordon Campbell's ministry he was convinced that the church was on the verge of a greater work. The night after his departure, another half-night of prayer was held for guidance about the next minister. One year later, Robert Allen was inducted. In the last ten years the church has doubled in numbers, and grown in love and caring. The half-nights have recently been resumed, particularly when seeking the Lord's will in specific situations.

persist in his intercession and call on the name of Yahweh. There was an enormous personal cost, yet Moses was transformed as a by-product of his intercession.

Paga

The word which is usually rendered 'intercession' in the Old Testament is the Hebrew word *paga*. This is a strong word and means 'a meeting with an outcome'. It has several Old Testament uses other than 'a meeting with God to pray for others' and these other uses help to build a full understanding of intercession.

The boundary

Paga is used in Joshua 19:11, 22, 26, 27 and 34 as the word to describe the meeting of one tribal boundary with another, at the furthest extent of a territory. The tribe could go to the *paga* and no further. This suggests that intercession is as far as we can go. There is no higher Court of Appeal. Under English Common Law a legal decision can be appealed against several times, but once the House of Lords has made its decision there can be no further legal action. We can do no more once we have interceded. Intercession is our spiritual boundary. In Genesis 18:16–33, when Abraham had finished interceding, the matter was closed. He returned home to await the verdict. What torment and sadness he must have felt when he saw the smoke—Genesis 19:28! Yet there was no more he could have done. He had reached the boundary. He had interceded.

Violence

Paga is also used to describe a violent meeting. It is used in Judges 8:21, 15:12, 1 Samuel 22:17–18, 2 Samuel 1:15, 1 Kings 2:25, 29, 31, 34 and 46 as the word for a meeting that ends in death. This is the same word which describes a man's meeting with God for prayer! It is a fearful thing to meet the living God, for no man can see God and live. Yet the intercessor is called into the presence of God to plead and argue. No Old Testament intercessor could be sure he would survive this encounter with God. In Genesis 32:24–32 it cost Jacob a dislocated hip.

In Jeremiah 7:16 *paga* is contrasted with other forms of prayer. Jeremiah was first told not to *palal*—habitually pray—for the people. Then he was instructed not to *rinnah*—cry loudly—for them. Next he was ordered not to *tephillah*—sing praises—about them. Finally, as the end of the matter, Jeremiah was commanded not to *paga* for them. He must not wrestle violently with God on their behalf.

Begging

Paga is used as the strongest Old Testament form of asking. It is often translated as 'entreat'. This presents a picture of begging for something that is desperately wanted. Abraham, in Genesis 23:8, asked the sons of Heth to *paga* with Ephron for the cave at Machpelah so that he could bury Sarah there. Through this intercession, the first piece of Canaan, the promised land, came into the ownership of God's chosen family. In Ruth 1:16 Ruth told Naomi not to *paga* her to turn back. Ruth, by her inspired resistance to Naomi's intercession, was able to enter into the territory of God and his people. One direct consequence was her marriage to Boaz. King David was their great grandson.

Prophets

Prophets were the intercessors of the Old Testament and by their anointing with the Spirit they had the right of access to God's face which was essential for this work. Genesis 20:7, which is the first reference to a prophet, reveals this link. King Abimelech is shown as understanding that the prophet Abraham had the right to intercede with God on behalf of the life of another. Jeremiah 15:11 presents intercession as part of the true service of a prophet. Jethro, in Exodus 18:19, suggested to Moses that he should make intercession his priority and Numbers 27:5 shows that Moses, who is the supreme prophet of the Old Testament, implemented this advice. Isaiah 59:16 reveals God's sadness at the absence of prophets to intercede with him. Joel 2:28–29 is a glorious prophecy that one day all God's people will prophesy—and thus all will be able to intercede. That day dawned at Pentecost. Through Christ's atoning work at Calvary we have gained the right of access to the Father's face. Through Christ's baptizing work at Pentecost we can receive the power to intercede.

The Old Testament prophets needed to receive either the word of the Lord or the Spirit of the Lord before they could prophesy. They dared not initiate a prophetic message. This also applied to intercession. Jeremiah 27:18 shows that the prophets who had received the word of the Lord were the ones who should have been interceding. We should not choose the object or occasion of our intercession. We should intercede only when God commands, and only about those matters that he reveals to us, by his word or by his Spirit.

Enteuxis

The Greek word *enteuxis* is usually translated as 'intercession' in the New Testament. It was in common use as the word to describe a petition to a king about another man, and was absorbed into the church to describe the Old Testament idea of *paga* praying. It is a gentler word than *paga*. Whereas *paga* was a meeting followed by an outcome, *enteuxis* was a meeting followed by a conversation. This word occurs seven times in the New Testament. Hebrews 7:25 and Romans 8:34 describe the work of Christ as the eternal Intercessor for the saints, in fulfilment of Isaiah 53:12. Romans 8:26–27 shows the work of the Holy Spirit in intercession as the partial fulfilment of Zechariah

12:10. These verses are examined on pages 25-34.

Loud protests

Acts 25:24 uses intercession in its technical sense. Festus stated that the whole Jewish community interceded with him, 'loudly protesting'. Intercession is not necessarily a quiet, private or orderly activity. The Jews were all simultaneously interceding with Festus for the death of Paul. This returns to the Old Testament link between intercession and violence. I feel less and less comfortable at the idea of Christ living evermore to intercede for me. He wants the death of my selfishness and disobedience. He grabs his father by the shoulders, gives a mighty shake and loudly protests about Tim Pain: 'Do something about him! Bring an end to his worldly thinking and idle living.' Amen.

I have experimented with a form of intercession which is better described as 'loud protests', in contrast to the more traditional 'whispered library' prayers. I call this 'simultaneous prayer'. All present are asked to intercede audibly, loudly and simultaneously about the same matter. This takes about five minutes or so in a meeting and is very powerful. We had to do that at many services before people gained confidence in God's ability to hear all the audible prayers at the same time. (Why did they not have the same problem with simultaneous silent prayer?)

Transformation

1 Timothy 4:5 follows the Old Testament idea that the word of God is the necessary prerequisite for intercession. This cannot be overstated. There is too much presumption in contemporary prayer. People sometimes assume that they have a general responsibility to pray for the whole world. This is not so. We need to recognize those matters which God has specially entrusted to us for intercession, and restrict ourselves to them. We do not have a general duty of intercession. We only have a particular duty to pray about those matters which God presents to us.

In 1 Timothy 4:5 the result of such intercession was total transformation. That which had been deemed evil became holy. One of our major objectives in intercession should be the consecration of the saints. Intercession should be engaged in to bring about the complete setting apart of God's people for service. This will be examined later.

Service

Romans 11:2 is a reference to the prophet Elijah's intercession described in 1 Kings 19:10–18. His intercession was a complaint to God about the behaviour of Israel. Elijah hoped for some action as the result of his praying, but instead he received a revelation. God was not going to do anything. Elijah had to do something. He must find and anoint Hazael, Jehu and Elisha. God often refuses to grant answers to prayer; instead he gives replies. We intercede with God: 'Do something about it,' we say, and he replies, 'No. You do this about it.' This is the secret of the miracle of the Cana wedding and the miracles of feeding the multitudes. The intercessor must listen whilst interceding and be ready to receive some instructions from God to perform a particular act of divine service.

Ministry of love

Intercession is the natural expression of a life filled to overflowing with the love of God. William Law suggested that intercession was 'an act of universal love'.[4] Jesus taught that we should love one another in the same manner as he has loved us (John 13:34–35). Christ expresses his love by living evermore to make intercession for us. If we are to love in his way, intercession must become a priority in our lives. This means that the level of our intercession is one measure of our loving. Intercession and love are inseparable. I discover a fresh zeal to pray, and new depths in prayer, whenever my children are ill. Why? Because I love them. As I write this first draft, my fourteen-month twins still wake nightly at least ten times each, between 7pm and 5.30am. God has spoken to me in this situation. He asks, 'Tim, why do you rise from your sleep to care for them, yet will not get out of your bed to intercede for others?' I find it most uncomfortable to be under the searchlight of a divine cross-examination.

Matthew 7:12, Luke 10:25–28 and 1 John 4:7–21 all unite in demanding our love for our brothers and sisters. Intercession is frequently the best and most useful way of expressing this love. Our power to do visible deeds of love and goodness is restricted. There are few people to whom we can contribute material help. Yet if our lives are full of loving intercession, God attributes to us the good works, the acts of love, about which we sincerely and honestly intercede, and would have performed had it been in our power. Just as the man who lusts after a woman in his heart is deemed to be an adulterer, so, too, God reckons to us those things we have longed for often, and brought about through our intercessions. We cannot heal all the sick, feed all the starving, comfort all the bereaved, but if we help those people God commands us to help, we can then go on to accomplish so much more in intercession.

There is a delightful side-effect in this intercession of love. As we pray for others to be changed, we are changed ourselves. The principle that those who forgive others themselves receive forgiveness applies in intercession. As we pour out our lives in heavenly love and holy intercession, so we are cleansed and purified, as by holy fire. The discipline of intercession brings an inevitable control upon our tongue. As we intercede for the blessing of others, for the knowledge of God's love to fill them, for their deliverance from imprisoning circumstances, so these thoughts become our natural attitudes and wishes for others. There is nothing that makes me love a man so much as praying for him. Once we start to intercede for a person, it is very hard to be other than at peace with him. In intercession, we begin to allow God to cement his love between us, not by worldly compatibility, but by the mutual communication of spiritual blessings in prayer. Through intercession Christians could gain such an incredible love for each other that they could become the eighth wonder of the world.

The Intercession of Jesus

The practice of Jesus

Jesus was a man of prayer. He rose early to pray and remained awake late to pray. He can be seen in prayer at every stage of his ministry. He prayed at his baptism, Luke 3:21, and after much ministry, Mark 1:35, 6:46, Luke 5:16. He prayed for a complete night before selecting the inner group of twelve disciples, Luke 6:12. Sometimes he prayed alone in the presence of his disciples, Luke 9:28–29. He prayed at the last supper, John 17, and in Gethsemane, Luke 22:41, Mark 14:32. He prayed at the crucifixion, Luke 23:34, and after his resurrection, Luke 24:30.

Jesus was and is 'the Intercessor'. Romans 8:34 states, 'He not only died for us—he rose from the dead, and there at God's right hand he stands and pleads for us.' Hebrews 7:25 declares, 'He is living for ever to intercede for all who come to God through him.' These two verses reveal the eternal activity of the resurrected Christ. As I write this, as you read this, as we live, and on till we die, Christ continues to intercede for us. His everlasting intercession for the saints is both a comforting and uncomfortable subject for meditation. These verses teach us that Jesus Christ lives essentially in heaven, not in human hearts. How sad it is to hear new believers talk of having invited Jesus into their hearts. If that were so, he could not intercede at the Father's right hand for them. No, the glorious truth is that we receive the Spirit into our lives at regeneration, and believe in the Christ who rules in the heavenly places. He is there to engage in this everlasting agonizing with the Father.

Romans 8:34 and Hebrews 7:25 show Christ as praying for the saints, for those who have come to God through him. This is a most important principle. We have no record of Jesus interceding for unbelievers and Paul does not instruct his readers to pray for those who are not Christians. Yet as I read contemporary literature on prayer, and take part in prayer groups, I receive the impression that the Scriptures must urge upon me the practice of praying for the salvation of unbelievers. This is not the case. The biblical emphasis is entirely upon intercession for the saints. Doubtless there will be those who would suggest that I am arguing from silence. I am not. I am simply revealing a silence that most people appear not to notice. The biblical material on intercession is in direct contrast with our contemporary practice. People major on interceding for the unsaved, whereas the Scriptures stress the priority of interceding for the saved. These people justify their prayers by espousing a zeal for evangelism, yet one can hardly say that Paul and Jesus lacked evangelistic zeal! This is discussed in more detail on page 36.

These two verses, Romans 8:34 and Hebrews 7:25, also stress the importance of persistence. If Christ needs to intercede without pause, how much more must we press on in prayer.

Jesus taught much about prayer, expressing in words the truths that his life demonstrated. He taught the disciples to pray privately and plainly, Matthew 6:5–9; to make definite daily requests, Matthew 6:11; and to ensure that they had forgiven everyone, Matthew 6:14–15, Luke 11:3–4. He told the disciples to pray with persistence, Luke 11:5–13, Luke 18:1–8; and with penitence, Luke 18:9–14. He instructed them in the twin secrets of asking in his name, John 14:13–

Kay Lepper—a member of Beulah Baptist Church, Bexhill, E. Sussex

Kay is a housebound, disabled spinster in her seventies, unable to attend church; nevertheless, she is an intercessor. She was converted in 1944 and two incidents soon taught her lasting lessons about intercession.

In one church service she was overwhelmed by a conviction that her father, though fit and healthy, would die within a month and she must win him for the Lord. She prayed rather a lot! As he was about to board an aeroplane, she gave him a Christian book. He was seated between two clergymen and one, like Philip speaking to the eunuch, asked about the book and then led him to salvation on the plane. One month later he had a heart attack and died.

Then Kay had a serious operation and was immobile in a plaster jacket for months. She filled her days with methodically praying around the world for the Oriental Missionary Society and felt God was using her prayers. Years went by and prayer was a lesser priority until she retired early because of her disablement. At that time, 1969, she was baptized in Holy Spirit and suddenly intercession became real again.

Kay recalled her early lessons and resolved to fill her remaining years with prayer. Whilst praying over a letter from a disabled friend she found herself speaking a string of sentences in tongues and realized the value of tongues in intercession.

Today Kay intercedes for three hours a day, receiving requests from her church tapes and other prayer letters. She says, 'I discuss each case with the Lord, asking him to show me how to pray. I sit quietly, listening and looking, waiting for the Lord to speak. After a while he suggests a scripture or similar incident from the past and says, "Pray along these lines." People often ring me with an urgent request, and sometimes in this listening I am given a message to pass on. I always press on till the result, but often it takes a long time. I find intercession strangely strengthening and most fulfilling.'

14, 26, John 16:23–24, 26, and of faith, Matthew 21:22.

The parable of Jesus

Jesus' clearest teaching on intercession is found in Luke 11:1–13. The disciples had seen him at prayer and asked to be taught how to pray. Jesus answered with a prayer to use, a parable to understand and some principles to follow. The parable of the persistent friend, in verses 5–8, teaches much about intercession. Here, the One who lives for ever to intercede reveals the necessary elements of this act of love.

The immediate need

Intercession has its origin in the unexpected arrival of an urgent need at an inconvenient time. We need only intercede when God presents us with a need, or burden, that must be dealt with, but we need to continue to intercede until it has been dealt with. God chooses the time for the commencement of our intercession, not us. The immediate need for which Christ prays is the state of his bride.

The necessary relationship

Intercession is the loving response of a person to his friend's need. In Jesus' parable, one man called on his friend who, in turn, called on another friend. We are friends of Jesus, John 15:13–15, and we intercede primarily for those who are our friends. It is the 'Jerusalem first' principle. Christ intercedes for those who come to God through him—for his friends.

The obvious love

In Luke 11:5–8, the man took his tired and hungry friend into his home. He did not make the excuse of an empty freezer or the late hour. He gave up his night's sleep, the comfort of his warm bed and risked his popularity with another friend to get some bread for his uninvited guest. Love is the motivating force of all intercession. True love gets us out of our beds and on to our knees. Christ intercedes because of his great love for his bride.

The helpless state

The man had no resources of his own with which to feed his friend. Great love can be utterly impotent. Parents may love their sick children, but still be unable to help them. The man was willing to provide from his own cupboard, but it was bare. This helplessness sent him begging to one whom he believed could meet the need. It is only the man who accepts his own weakness who can receive the strength of God. Christ intercedes because there is nothing else he can do. He has laid down his life, shed his blood, risen from the dead, ascended to the Father and baptized his bride in Holy Spirit. He can do only one more thing: finally, he intercedes with his Father.

The prayer of faith

The intercessor was sure his friend would help. He knew his friend would not mind being woken at midnight. His faith took him into the dark and the cold. It is this faith which makes intercession purposeful. Scripture shows God as poised, ready and eager to deliver good things, especially the Holy Spirit, to those who ask. The astonishing promises of John 14:16 should lead to a confident faith that causes intercessory prayer to pour from our lips. Jesus has absolute confidence that his Father will hear his prayer. He knows his intercession is not in vain. His prayers for the bride will be answered.

The vital persistence

But the man's hopes were quickly dashed. His rich friend would not help. This is the point of the parable. Intercession is surrounded by difficulties and delays. God wants us—I do not know why—to persevere. The application of the parable in verses 9–13 uses a Greek tense which is best understood as 'keep on asking, keep on seeking, keep on knocking'. If the man persists, he will get his bread. If he gives up, he will return home empty-handed. Jesus keeps on interceding for us. Nothing will make him stop.

The certain result

However, it all ended happily. The man eventually got the three loaves. It does not matter whether he obtained it because of his relationship, or because of his persistence. What counts is the bread in his hands. Some suggest that Jesus implicitly contrasted the rich friend of verse 8 with the heavenly Father in verse 13. This underlines the certainty of a result in intercession. Disappointment is impossible with our Friend, the Father. Jesus' prayers will not be frustrated. His bride will be made ready for the wedding.

The prayer of Jesus

Jesus concluded the last supper discourse, where he had taught much about the Holy Spirit and prayer, with his high priestly prayer, which is recorded in John 17. This prayer is our clearest example of Christ's intercession. If Matthew 6:9–13 is our model prayer, then John 17 must be our model intercession.

John 17 divides into three prayers. Verses 1–8 record Jesus praying for himself. This is not intercession, but we can learn from these verses how we can ask others to pray for us. Verses 9–19 show Jesus praying for the eleven disciples, and in verses 20–26, he intercedes for us.

Five features are common to these three prayers:

(a) Each prayer begins with a precise statement showing for whom Jesus is praying (verses 1, 9, 20).

(b) Each prayer has glory as a main theme (verses 1–5, 10, 22).

(c) Each prayer is addressed to the Father (verses 5, 11, 21).

(d) Each prayer mentions the men given to Jesus by the Father (verses 2, 9, 24).

(e) Each prayer contains the theme of Jesus' proclamation to men about the Father (verses 6, 14, 26).

Jesus' prayer for himself

His great cry was that the Son would be glorified so that he could effectively glorify the Father. Dr Raymond Brown (the Roman Catholic, not the Baptist) has defined glory as 'a visible manifestation of majesty through acts of power'.[5] We should cry out for the Father to glorify the Son in us. This is the function of the Holy Spirit. We should intercede for him to increase his work in our lives. Calvary and Easter morning were the consequences of Christ's request for glory. Suffering and transformation often come in the wake of intercession.

Jesus had revealed the Father's name to the twelve disciples. In John's Gospel, with its emphasis on revealing Jesus as the divine Son of God, the name of God is an important theme. It seems that John understood this name to be *ego eimi*—'I am what I am', or perhaps, 'I will be what I will be'. To reveal the name of God is to reveal his nature. Jesus had revealed the name of God by revealing himself as God. There is a mystery here which will never be unveiled, not even when he comes again in glory (Revelation 19:12). Today, Jesus is known by the name *Jesus*. He can also be identified by the names *The Word of God* (Revelation 19:13) and *The King of kings and the Lord of lords* (Revelation 19:16) but he has another name which is known by no man. It is this secret name and the three hundred and more other known names of God that we hint at when we pray 'in the name of Jesus'. Every time we pray in his 'name', we anticipate the end of this age. Deuteronomy 12:5, Psalm 9:7–10, Psalm 20:7, Psalm 22:22 and Isaiah 52:6 all look forward to that day. The work of proclaiming and revealing God's divine name and nature should be one subject of our intercession.

Jesus' prayer for the Eleven

This prayer is an extension of his own prayer for glorification. It is in the perseverance and witness of the disciples that the name of God will be glorified. Opposition is a theme of the prayer. The disciples are to be left in the world, but they do not belong to it. They are aliens and, therefore, they will provoke trouble. Jesus has given them God's word, so the world will react with inevitable hatred. It is what Jesus does not pray in this situation which is particularly instructive. Jesus does not pray for the world and he does not pray for the hostility to cease. Instead, his prayer is for safety. Verse 11 says, 'Keep them safe, by the power of your name, the name you gave me.' (GNB.) It is a common Old Testament idea that the name of God is both the place and the means of safety. Psalm 20, Psalm 91:14, Psalm 124 and Proverbs 18:10 all illustrate this. We often pray for an easy option when God wants to reveal his depth of love in the face of adversity. Christ could not leave the world without facing the Evil One. Neither can we. We should pray for safety and strength, not for the cessation of any opposition.

Jesus did pray positively for the Eleven. He asked that they be set apart—consecrated—for service, and set apart in the truth. This must, following on from John 15:26–27, be a setting apart in the Holy Spirit, that Spirit of truth, for service. We should earnestly plead for the believers God has burdened us to pray for, that they be consecrated in the Spirit for action. This is real intercession for evangelism. Instead of praying for people to be saved we pray for those who have been saved. We pray that they will serve God more and more by proclaiming his name to those who do not know him.

Jesus' prayer for us

Christ offered two prayers on our behalf. He prayed, firstly, that we would be one. The Holy Trinity is the model for this

Two examples from history

In 1722 the remaining few persecuted Moravian Christians found safety in Saxony on the estate of Count Zinzendorf. He allowed them to build the village of Herrnhut.

Sadly, there followed five years of bickering, but on May 12th 1727 God poured out his Holy Spirit upon them and they were transformed as they were filled with his love. They resolved that the sacred fire on the altar of prayer must never go out and established a twenty-four-hour-a-day prayer chain which continued for over one hundred years.

As the result of an unexpected meeting in 1732 with a West Indian slave, Zinzendorf initiated the greatest missionary movement ever seen. Leonard Dober, a potter, and David Nitschmann, a carpenter, were the pioneers. They left Herrnhut in August to work their passage to the West Indies. By 1747, missionaries had gone from Herrnhut to every continent and had won over three thousand converts. In 1757, the hundredth missionary left the small village, and by 1832 there were forty-five thousand converts in forty-one countries.

In 1857, Jeremiah Lamphier believed God was moving him to arrange a united meeting for prayer on Wednesdays at noon in New York city. He arranged a suitable hall but when he went there at the announced time, no one else came. By 12.30 pm he had concluded that he had been misguided. However, by 1 o'clock six others had joined him. The following Wednesday there were twenty, the week after, forty, and within six months ten thousand business men were meeting daily for prayer in New York! Within two years, two million converts had been added to the church in America.

In August 1859, a united prayer meeting began in London and soon there were a hundred men meeting daily at noon. By the November of that year, there were twenty daily and forty weekly prayer meetings. A wave of prayer swept Great Britain and by the end of 1861 one million converts were added to the churches in this country.

unity. It is a unity of diversity which has its origin in divine, not human, action. It is to be a visible unity to challenge the world about the deity of Christ. Jesus challenged the world by his obvious oneness with the Father. We will only challenge the world when we are one with each other and with the Godhead. Jesus also challenged the world by revealing God's glory in the acts of power he performed. We will only challenge the world when we do likewise. Signs and wonders are, therefore, inseparably intertwined with unity. The one is impossible without the other. If we want signs and wonders we should be interceding for oneness. It is interesting to note that the 'charismatic movement' within the historic churches has resulted, without any human manipulation, in this visible divine oneness; and that signs and wonders are beginning to be seen with increasing frequency. It is also worth noting that the Westminster 'Third Wave' Conference in 1984, which saw such an astonishing breakthrough in 'signs and wonders', was attended by a mixture of leaders who previously had shunned each other's company. House-church and denominational leaders rubbed shoulders, prayed and shared with each other for the first time, and gaped at the way this unity was blessed. Sadly, most do not seem to have grasped the cause and effect.

Jesus' second prayer for us was that we would be with him for ever. The Bridegroom is seen to be interceding for the rapid arrival of his wedding day. We know that the Spirit also cries, 'Come.' The question must be put: 'Is the bride crying out, "Come"?' It is a New Testament promise that after enduring the sufferings of this world we will see and enjoy the glory of God. Christ is hastening this day by his work of intercession. He calls us to share in it with him.

The Intercession of St Paul

Paul is introduced to us, in Acts 9:11, as a man at prayer. Prayer was the bedrock of his extraordinary ministry. Seven times he suggested that we should live in the way he lived (1 Corinthians 11:1; Galatians 4:12; Philippians 3:17; 4:9; 1 Thessalonians 1:6; 2 Thessalonians 3:7–9). If we are serious about the work of intercession, we must pay special attention to this mighty man of prayer and learn from his teaching and his praying.

Paul's teaching

Paul, in 1 Timothy 2:1–4, advised that the practice of prayer in Christian meetings should include petition, thanksgiving and intercessions. (Sadly, most non-Anglican churches ignore this advice.) Intercessions are to be offered vicariously on behalf of all men. We are urged to pray for them—in their stead—because they do not pray themselves. This we do as priests, as members of the royal priesthood; pleading with God on behalf of the world. This intercession should be on behalf of the government and have prime place in our services.

Paul was the apostle to the Gentiles. We have no record that he ever prayed for God to save them. Verse 4 shows

35

why: Paul knew that it was God's heart's desire to save them. He knew he need not waste time interceding for God to give salvation to the Gentiles, because God had already made it clear to Paul that this was what he wanted to do. Paul's intercessions for the unsaved are not that they be saved, but that the obstacles preventing their salvation be removed, and that the human messengers of their salvation be equipped. We will go into these two aspects of intercession for evangelism in some detail.

Paul's only recorded intercession for a group to be saved is found in Romans 10:1: 'I have the very warmest love for the Jews, and I pray to God for them to be saved.' This particular verse must be read in the context of Romans 9, 10 and 11, Paul's three great chapters on God's purpose for Israel. It cannot be taken as support for, 'Dear God, please save John' type prayers. Paul knew that the temporary blindness of the larger section of Israel was the means of the present salvation for the pagans. He equally believed that the present salvation of the pagans would bring about the future salvation of all Israel. Paul was confident that God wanted to save the Jews at some time in the future, but was not convinced that this was God's will for the present. This meant there was a reality and purpose in Paul's wrestling with God that the Israelites 'may be saved', but he need not do this for the Gentiles.

In 1 Timothy 2:1–4 Paul taught that our vicarious priestly intercession on behalf of the government should be, 'that we may be able to live religious and reverent lives in peace and quiet'. Peace is crucial for the effective proclamation of the gospel. War is an obstacle to evangelism. We pray for peace so that God's work may not be disrupted, and that we may continue with the task of witnessing to those who do not believe.

Paul passed on Christ's teaching of the necessity for perseverance in prayer. Romans 12:12, Ephesians 6:18, Colossians 4:2 and 1 Thessalonians 5:17 all emphasize the need to continue in prayer. He stressed that prayer should be for absolute priorities, not for luxuries. Ephesians 6:18 and Philippians 4:6–7 teach that we should ask and pray only for what we need. This echoes Matthew 6:25–34. Paul even went into details about a right posture in prayer. I find it amazing that there has been so much acrimony in the last twenty years when 1 Timothy 2:8 is so explicit.

Paul's prayer requests

In addition to his frequent injunction to 'pray for us', Paul made seven detailed prayer requests. Four themes run through these requests for prayer.

Rescue

Six times Paul asked for prayer that he would be kept safe in, or rescued from, a situation which was preventing the proclamation of the gospel. He obeyed Christ in asking not for the hostilities to cease but for safety as he walked away from the difficulty. This means that in our prayers we should focus on the saints rather than on their circumstances. We should see what God is doing, and wants to do, with them, rather than be side-tracked by looking at the surrounding events and praying for the situation. Paul asked to be rescued from evil men, 2 Thessalonians 3:1–2; from unbelievers, Romans 15:31; and from a deadly peril, 2 Corinthians 1:9–11. He asked to be kept safe in prison, Philippians 1:19–20, and to be released from prison as a special favour, Philemon 22. Finally, he asked that a closed door be opened, Colossians 4:3. In all these verses Paul's request was made in order to enable him to witness more effectively.

Acceptance

In 2 Thessalonians 3:1–2 Paul requested prayer that the message he spoke would be well received by unbelievers; and in Romans 15:30–32 that his message would prove acceptable to the Jerusalem believers.

Battle Baptist Church, E. Sussex

Reg and Eva Boorman joined this country church in 1934 when it was at a peak of growth. It had a young minister who was fresh from college and full of ideas; the evening congregation numbered sixty and there was a thriving Sunday School. But three years later the minister had left, the church was in debt and the spiritual tide had turned. In the next forty-four years Reg and Eva saw that tide disappear over the horizon until, in 1978, the evening service closed, having slumped to four attenders. Throughout those long years, Reg and Eva had interceded. They prayed at home and at church. Reg even prayed on his rounds as the local postman.

In 1943, Reg was filled with the Holy Spirit, given the gift of tongues, and a compelling vision that God would do something great in their church. In the late 1940s, he saw the local Congregational church first close its weekly prayer meeting, then be forced to shut down completely. Reg became convinced that Battle Baptist Church would also close if its weekly prayer meeting ended. It did not, as Reg and Eva prayed on. Even when only four turned up, they continued in intercession, based on his 1943 vision. Sometimes their faith wavered, but always the Spirit moved them back to prayer. For forty-four years they interceded for revival in Battle. Their prayer was short and simple: 'Revive us, O Lord.'

Their first encouragement came in 1979, when a young part-time pastor was appointed. Four months later, he tragically died. The Boormans prayed on and suddenly, for no clear reason, the tide turned. A new part-time minister came, faith grew, the Holy Spirit sent his gifts. People began to be converted and by 1985 the re-opened evening service regularly attracted fifty attenders—sometimes over a hundred. Reg and Eva have seen God do something great in their small church. It has taken a long time, but he has kept his word, because they have faithfully persevered in intercession.

Boldness

In both Ephesians 6:19–20 and Colossians 4:3–4 Paul asked for prayer for fearless boldness. He wanted to speak the good news as it should be spoken. He knew his normal state was 'fear and trembling' and that boldness did not come naturally to him. If Paul needed people's prayers for boldness, how much more must this feature in our intercessions today.

Travel

Paul requested prayer, in Romans 15:22–32, for an opportunity to travel to Rome. He asked this so that he could take a blessing from Christ to the Romans.

These four themes in Paul's prayer requests suggest much that can help us in interceding for evangelism. If our passion is the biblical passion for evangelism, how do we best pray for our unbelieving friends and family? It does not seem to me that 'Dear God, please save John' prayers are either biblically based or empirically effective. If we follow Paul (and who better to follow?) we will intercede for Sam Believer to be rescued from the imprisoning circumstances preventing his witness, to be filled with great boldness to speak God's word, kept safe to travel and spend time with John, and that Sam's message to John Unbeliever will prove acceptable in his ears. 'Dear God, please save John' prayers are lazy prayers. We need to listen to God to establish who he wants to bring his promised salvation to John, and then we can intercede specifically and persistently for God to remove the obstacles, to equip the saint he has chosen to speak to John, and empower the words with his grace and favour.

Let me make it quite plain what I am, and am not, saying. I am not saying prayer has no part in evangelism. I am not saying that God will never honour the sincere motives of those who pray 'God, please save John'. Sovereign God cannot be imprisoned in a straitjacket by my sentences or another's prayers. I am not saying that all those prayers for the salvation of the world are of necessity a waste of time, but I am saying that they are not the most effective prayers for realizing that promise of salvation.

Intercession is a subsection of prophecy and, as such, divine instructions need to be received before the activity commences. The particular person that God wants to save must be established through prophetic listening. Then the saint whom God wants to use as the human messenger to that individual should be identified by quiet seeking. The intercessions for that saintly messenger should then begin along the lines already suggested of rescue from circumstances, boldness to speak, safe travel and acceptable words.

Paul's intercessions

Nine of Paul's intercessory prayers, not including his doxologies, are recorded in Holy Scripture. These contain a wealth of material to guide our intercession.

Knowledge

Paul's most frequent prayer was that the saints be filled with whatever knowledge he understood them to need. He prayed that the Ephesians would know Jesus better by receiving the Spirit of wisdom and revelation, Ephesians 1:17; that they would know the hope to which they had been called by receiving enlightenment, Ephesians 1:18; that they would know the riches of Christ's inheritance, Ephesians 1:18; and, finally, that they would know the vastness of Christ's love, Ephesians 3:18. He prayed for the Colossians that they would know the will of God by receiving wisdom and understanding, Colossians 1:9; and that they would grow in the knowledge of God, Colossians 1:10. He asked God that the Romans would know the righteousness which comes from God and be able to distinguish it from their own righteousness, Romans 10:1–4. He prayed for Philemon, Apphia, Archippus and the church that met in his house, that they would know every good thing that was available to them in Christ, Philemon 6. Finally, Paul interceded for the Philippians that they would have greater knowledge so that they could discern what was best, Philippians 1:9-10.

Paul used the Greek word *epignosis* in all but two of these passages. This means a full, experiential knowledge. He interceded with God for them to experience these things in as full and complete a manner as was possible. One exception is Ephesians 3:18. Here he used *gnosis* which signifies a grasp of the concept rather than of the detail. The vast love of God cannot be known fully and completely, even though it can be enjoyed and appreciated. The other exception is Ephesians 1:18a, where Paul used the Greek word *oida* to stress that the hope is a present understanding of a future reality. The hope will come to pass, but it cannot be known fully and completely at the present time.

Before we begin to intercede for a person, we should ask God, 'What knowledge does this believer most need?' And then wait for the answer before we start to pray for them. Paul was always specific in his intercessions for knowledge. They varied with different needs. Our intercessions must develop into this real prayer struggle for the saints, that they will know, fully and completely, all they need to know to help them in their evangelism.

Strength

Paul prayed in Ephesians 3:16 that the saints might be made strong with power through the Spirit. This was so that eventually (therefore it could not have happened at conversion!) they would be made strong enough for Christ to dwell in their hearts and it was linked with being filled with the utter fullness of God. When will we be strong enough for this to take place? He prayed in Colossians 1:11 that they would be made powerful with the power of God's might for endurance and patience. When someone is in danger of giving up, we should not pray that things will become easier. Instead, we should pray that the Spirit will make them powerful and resolute to press on. Paul also prayed in 1 Thessalonians 3:13 that their hearts would be made firm so they might be blameless and holy at the second coming of Christ. These prayers for strength should feature in our intercessions for each other, so that we can be strong for evangelism.

Love

Paul interceded for the Ephesians that God's love might be their root and foundation, Ephesians 3:17. He begged that God's love might flow out to them over and above their present experience, and overflow to others, Philippians 1:9, 1 Thessalonians 3:12. This love, being God's love, is *agape*. It is God's deep, constant and practical love. We need to pray much for this in today's church, that *agape* may abound and overflow. It is this love, after all, which will challenge the world.

Pure and blameless

In Philippians 1:10 Paul prayed that the saints would become 'pure and blameless' before men. He wanted God to make them *eilikrines* and *aproskopos*—that is, pure and untainted by the world, not giving anybody offence or a reason for stumbling. Paul interceded for balanced Christian living. He prayed in 1 Thessalonians 3:13 that the saints would be 'pure and blameless' before God. This time he interceded for them to be *amemptos* and *hagiosune*—to be blameless before God and holy in their personal conduct. He also asked in Colossians 1:10, that their lives might give pleasure to God. This is reminiscent of the Old Testament description of Enoch as someone who pleased God. Paul wanted them not merely to keep God's commands, but to anticipate his wishes. It is the difference between, one day, me telling my daughter to tidy her bedroom and, another day, returning home to find it already done. Finally, he interceded for their 'perfection', 2 Corinthians 13:9. This is *katartisis* not *teleios*. It is a realistic prayer for them to be ready or fit for evangelistic action. It is not a prayer for complete maturity or total perfection.

Worthy

Paul wanted his readers to live in such a way that they would reflect God's character and thoughts. So, in Colossians 1:10, he prayed that they would live worthily towards the Lord, and in 2 Thessalonians 1:11 he interceded for them to live worthy of God's calling.

Righteousness

In Philippians 1:11, Paul prayed that they would be filled with the fruit of righteousness that comes through Jesus. He also prayed, in Romans 10:2–3, that they would know the righteousness which comes from God.

Results

Paul interceded for his readers that they might bear fruit in good works, Colossians 1:10; and that they would be *energes*—powerfully active—and effective in sharing their faith, Philemon 6.

Glory

I would have been surprised if Paul, who so closely followed Jesus' pattern of intercession, had made no mention of the name and glory of God in his prayers for others. However, he did not deviate from his Master's example. 'We pray this so that the name of our Lord Jesus may be glorified in you, and you in him' (2 Thessalonians 1:12, NIV). Paul used the passive form to stress the present possibility of this, and underlined it by using the same construction in verse 10 to stress the future certainty of Christ's glorification in his bride.

Obstacle-Removing Intercession

I earlier suggested that intercession for the unsaved consisted of two elements, firstly that the human messengers be equipped—which we have examined—and secondly that the obstacles preventing their salvation be removed. It is this second aspect of intercession which we will now examine.

Jesus took the common Jewish phrase 'to move a mountain' and vested it with new power and application. In Jewish writings a great teacher, one who explained satisfactorily difficulties in Scripture, was described as a mountain-mover. This phrase has its scriptural base in Isaiah 40:1–5, where the prophet was told to prepare the way of the Lord. Amongst other things, Isaiah had to knock down the mountains of difficulty which were obstructing the widespread revelation of the glory of God. 'Mountain-moving is hinted at in Isaiah 2:11–16 and its counterpart of 'uprooting' is suggested in Lamentations 3:65–66. The idea also appears in Zechariah 4:7.

In olden days, when an Eastern monarch wanted to travel to distant parts of his kingdom, he would send a party of men, some six months to a year in advance, to prepare the way. These men would make good the bridges, repair the roads, uproot trees and generally do everything they could to facilitate the easy journeying and arrival of the monarch. John the Baptist was the preparer of the way of the Lord, but so also were the Seventy-two in Luke 10. They went ahead of Christ in pairs to all the towns and places he was to visit. Jesus took up the idea of 'mountain-moving' and developed it in three parallel passages, Matthew 17:20, Mark 11:22–24, and Luke 17:5–6. A distinctive form of intercession emerges from these verses, which I call 'obstacle-removing' intercession.

A right understanding of Mark 11:22 is crucial. Bad translations have led us astray. Every translation that I have read suggests that Jesus said, 'Have faith in God.' But in the Greek there is no preposition. The normal translation would lead us to expect an *en* or *eis* before 'God' with *Theos* in the accusative or dative. But there is no *eis* or *en* and *Theos* is in the genitive. We must correct our Bibles and write in, 'Be having faith of God.' This transforms Jesus' teaching. To have God's faith in us is quite different from putting our faith in God. God's faith is absolute. He is totally self-confident. He knows that he can achieve whatever he wants to do. Mountain-moving, or obstacle-removing, becomes a distinct possibility with this understanding. Matthew 17:20 and Luke 17:5–6 underline this. We do not need much faith to move mountains, just the genuine article. It is quality, not quantity, that counts.

Faith is like the clutch in a car. A car can be throbbing with power, engine racing, first gear engaged, but it will remain stationary as long as the foot stays on the clutch. All that is necessary to cause the power to be released is a slight movement of the driver's left foot. That is faith. We do not need much faith if the vehicle is in first class condition, but if it is a rusty wreck we will need phenomenal faith. Would moving the metaphorical equivalent of the Himalayas cause Almighty God any problems? I think not. All we need is a speck of his faith to be given to us. Paul promised, in 1 Corinthians 12:9, that the Holy Spirit would give the gift of God's faith to some people during the worship of their local church. Paul then went on to urge his readers to be zealous for, or to desire earnestly, the higher gifts (verse 31). Faith is high on the list.

I suggest that there are five stages in obstacle-removing intercession.

Knowing God's will

This intercession is futile without the absolute certainty of the knowledge of God's will. Time must be spent listening to the Father. We must receive his identification of the mountains of difficulty which are the obstacles preventing God's glory from being seen, and from the person being saved. We need to ask the Father what the circumstances, factors, people, attitudes, etc are which prevent the work of God from developing and growing in a person. Each of the Gospel passages mentioned above suggests a particular type of obstacle for removal. Mark implies that personal relationships, especially where unforgiveness exists, can be one barrier. Matthew hints that difficulty in casting out demons may require this type of intercession. Luke, if taken with other passages about the fig/mulberry trees, suggests that those trees which look good but have no fruit are ripe candidates for uprooting. Fruitless, hypocritical Christians are often the greatest obstacle to people becoming Christians.

Authoritative order

These verses do not say 'Whoever prays to me', but 'Whoever speaks to the mountain'. This intercession is addressed to the obstacle, not the Father. It is violent, Old Testament *paga* intercession: 'Be taken up'; 'Be cast into the sea'; 'Move hence'; 'Be rooted up'. This is only strange to some because of their lack of experience in the apostolic practice of uttering authoritative commands in ministry. Christians in the early church, and an increasing number today, spoke directly to eyes, limbs, storms, demons, fevers and dead bodies 'in the name of Jesus' and commanded them to be

Richard Barden—St Peter's, Ashburnham, E. Sussex

My wife and I moved to Ashburnham in July 1982. I immediately felt a God-given burden for Richard, the local young man who was employed as 'mower' in the grounds. I began by thanking God that he wanted to save Richard and asked him what I should do. No sooner had I begun praying than Richard's sister was converted. This was a real encouragement, but I felt my only instruction was to befriend him. I prayed for wisdom and boldness, but my attempts were misconstrued and Richard took a dislike to me. I next prayed that he would recognize the change in his sister, that she would be an effective witness, and I requested further guidance.

In May 1983, Harry, a local mechanic whom Richard admired and helped, was miraculously converted. He came for weekly discipling and I enlisted his help in interceding about Richard. I invited Richard, in September 1983, to join our Bible Study. He did so and played a lively part, but the group ended in January 1984 at our twins' birth.

Throughout 1984 Richard drifted from God. In prayer, God showed Harry and myself that this was due to the influence of his girlfriend and a work-mate. In December 1984 we received clear instructions to commence 'obstacle clearing' intercession, and on our knees we persistently ordered the work-mate and girlfriend to leave. Within three months they had gone of their own free will. Two months later, in May 1985, Richard asked to see me. He came and said that he must give his life totally to God. He did, and since then has been a shining witness for Christ. The ex-girlfriend was separately converted and they are now re-united.

changed. We often cry 'Do something', but God whispers back, 'No, you do it'. This is the secret of the healing of Naaman, the miraculous catches of fish, the parting of the Sea of Reeds and the Temple tax paid by Peter. This executive authority, which Christ gave to the Seventy-two in Luke 10:1–16, is ours to use today. This means in practice that, if the obstacle preventing John Unbeliever's conversion is revealed in prayer as David Barrier, a cynical workmate, it would be right to intercede as follows: 'David Barrier, I command you to be removed from John's place of work; in the name of God, Amen.'

Receiving God's faith

Home produced faith will be insufficient for this intercession. God-given confidence that this will happen is needed. When the Holy Spirit gives his gift of God's faith during worship, we are to accept the event as already being done. To believe is not to have a faint hope that something could, or might, take place, for example, 'I believe (but I am not really sure) James will come today.' To believe is to know for certain that it will happen: 'I believe (he has promised me—and there he is walking towards me) James will come today.'

Sustained speaking

The Greek tense used means that we are to go on saying to the obstacle, 'Get up and throw yourself in the sea.' It is not a one-off command. Perseverance, as with all intercession, is required. When the Ashburnham Stable Family began to 'move mountains' it took ten months of sustained speaking before we noticed the obstacles beginning to remove themselves.

Visible result

The grammatical construction of the phrases 'it will be done', 'it will move', 'it will obey', emphasizes the certainty of fulfilment. Luke uses a Greek tense which refers to a time prior to the command, for example, 'it would have obeyed' and this underlines the fact that there is to be a visible result to this intercession. When we know God's will, receive God's faith, and continue in speaking out an authoritative order, there can be no doubt about the outcome. The highest mountain, the most deeply rooted tree, the most immovable obstacle, all have to go. The way will be made level for the glory of God to be seen. John Unbeliever will be saved.

I have used obstacle-removing intercession for several years. I believe God identified many obstacles that needed to be removed and thrown into the English Channel because they were preventing particular individuals from turning to Christ. They have been varied—pride in a particular property; unbelief in a factory; drunkenness; occultism, spiritualism and freemasonry; several antagonistic individuals; unhelpful relationships. These have been, or still are being, commanded to 'be uprooted and go hence!' Some have gone. The rest are going.

Satan-Defeating Intercession

Not many Christians have been trained in Satan-defeating intercession. Few exercise the divine power which is available to demolish strong-holds (2 Corinthians 10:3–4). Still fewer know how to resist the devil so that they see him flee before them (James 4:7). Ephesians 6:10–18 is the passage we must examine to learn about this type of intercession. How many Christians live equipped and clothed with the full armour of God, to stand firm in the day of evil? We will not be effective intercessors until we have learnt to overcome Satan.

I believe the key to Ephesians 6:10–17 is to be found in verse 18. Prayer is not another piece of the armour, or else the analogy has broken down. Neither is prayer a development of the sword of the Spirit. Prayer enables us to use the armour. It is our contact point with the army of evil. Prayer is the battlefield. The Good News Bible comes closest to the feel of the original with, 'Do all this in prayer.' God's armour is to be used in intercession. In Isaiah 59:15–19 the Lord was so appalled that there was no one to intercede that he personally decided to intervene; but note what he equipped himself with first! There are hints of God wearing his own armour in Isaiah 11:4–5 and in the apocryphal book of Wisdom (5:17–23). We are both the body of Jesus and the army of Jesus. We need to wear his armour for intercession, and, unlike Saul's armour on David, it will be a perfect fit.

It is important to realize that the armour is to be put on only once. Paul used a Greek tense which shows that the 'putting on' is not to be a repeated activity. Many people make the mistake of trying to put on each piece of armour every morning. But they have no answer to the questions, 'Why did you take it off?' or 'When did you take it off?' It may be helpful to affirm daily that God has clothed us with his armour, but that is another matter.

Though the 'putting on' is once and for all, the 'be strong' is continuous. Paul used another tense to show that we are to grow stronger continually and to go on being strengthened with the strength of God's power. We do not pray for our own strength to be increased, but for it to be replaced by God's strength. It is God's strength we should petition for. It is also crucial to realize that it is not individuals who put on God's armour. It is the local church. Many have perpetuated the 1950s infatuation with the individual by assuming the bulk of the New Testament is addressed to 'me' when it is written to 'us'—the church. It is against the church that the gates of hell will not prevail (Matthew 16:18). No such promise exists for the isolated individual, however well dressed he may be.

The opposition

When a local church is fully clothed with the whole armour of God it can go on being strengthened so as to stand against all the *methodeia*—cunning devices, methods—of the evil one. We are called to be involved in the 'wrestling' of verse 12. This is not long distance, push-button warfare, but a face to face grappling, with sweaty bodies intertwined and groaning. This is Old Testament *paga* intercession, with an implicit cross-reference to Genesis 32:24–32. Jacob wrestled with God and survived. The church is called to wrestle with Satan and stand her ground.

Paul described the opposition in four words. *Arche*—this is the first tier of demon rulers. They are those with authority over a specific locality, as seen in Daniel 10:12–21. *Exousia*—these are roving demons with freedom of action and a right to act in the world against believers. *Kosmokrator*—this is the highest level of demon rulers. It is the position which was offered to Jesus in Matthew 4:9. They control the world. *Poneria*—this is the malign army of evil in the heavenlies. These are the demonic 'vultures' who hover over the landscape of humanity.

This is a real battle. Only the church, clothed with God's armour, can wrestle with these powerful beings with any expectation of standing her ground.

The equipment

Many make much of defensive and offensive weapons. Dr Martyn Lloyd-Jones wrote that there are five defensive weapons and a sword which is both defensive and offensive.[6] I believe that all the armour is defensive. The language of Ephesians 6:10–17 is the language of spiritual survival. We resist, not attack; we stand our ground, not push forward. The devil has no greater aim than to stop Christians praying. The armour is given to ensure that he does not succeed. As we move towards prayer, so the devil comes to wrestle with us to prevent us from praying.

We have the belt of truth to protect us from lies like, 'God won't hear you'; the breastplate of righteousness to save us from giving up when he whispers, 'You can't pray. Remember what you thought yesterday. You're a worthless sinner'; the army boots of eager readiness to spread the gospel, with which to stamp on temptations not to bother to pray for guidance or boldness: 'Do it tomorrow,' he says. The huge four feet by two and a half feet shield, almost the size of a front door, with layer upon layer of skins soaked in water, to extinguish immediately these flaming darts of doubt: 'This will not work. There will be no change. You are wasting your time.' The crash helmet to help us keep on praying when a stunning blow falls—illness, accident, redundancy, bereavement, etc. The armour does not place us in a war-free zone; it enables us to survive in a holocaust. The knockout blow gives a headache instead of a broken skull. Psalm 124 puts this in sharp focus.

If the devil cannot stop us from praying, he will try to distract us with temptations. We are to use the defensive sword of the word of God to fight off the temptations of ambition and grandeur, as Christ did in the wilderness (Matthew 4:1–11). The 'word' is the Greek word *rhema*, not *logos*. This is not limited to the Bible. *Rhema* refers to a spoken word and can be either a scriptural quotation or an inspired prophetic utterance, or both. Thomas à Kempis illustrated this in *The Imitation of Christ*, where his advice on defeating Satan in prayer is a mixture of both Scripture and prophecy.

> Say to him. 'Away, unclean spirit! Blush for shame, wretch. You are foul indeed to speak of these things! Off with you, most evil of liars. You shall have no part in me. Jesus will be with me like a mighty warrior, and you will stand confounded. I would rather die and suffer any torture than consent to you. Be silent, and shut your mouth! I will listen to you no longer, however often you pester me. The Lord is my light and my salvation: whom shall I fear? Though a host encamp against me, my heart shall not be afraid. The Lord is my helper and redeemer.'[7]

Having done all this and stood firm, we are to pray at all times in the Spirit. When we have wrestled with Satan, and stood our ground in the face of his temptations not to engage in intercession, we are to, 'Pray all the time, asking for what you need, praying in the Spirit on every possible occasion. Never get tired of staying awake to pray for all the saints; and pray for me....' Intercession should be the church's continuous, never-ending activity.

Unceasing Intercession

This is an important practice for the Ashburnham Stable Family. We believe God has called us to maintain an unbroken chain of intercession for revival and renewal in East Sussex. The Stable has been a place for prayer since 1969, but on April 1st, 1978 we consecrated ourselves to intercede by night and day, 365 days a year, until the Lord Jesus returns in power and great glory. It was through our reading of Isaiah 62 that we came to believe that God wanted to set us as watchmen on the walls of the East Sussex church. We were to watch for those seeking to attack, those seeking to enter, and be ready at all times to sound the alarm. We were not to be silent by day or night. These Ashburnham Insight books are one consequence of our intercession. They are 'sounding the alarm' about the increasing stranglehold new traditions have on renewal. Luis Palau's dictum, 'Back to the Bible or back to the jungle' applies to charismatics as well as those to whom it was originally aimed.

I suggest that Isaiah 62 shows that God wants to set remembrancers in the church, people who, in intercession, will continually remind God of his promises and urge him to intervene. They are to take no rest, nor allow God any peace or quiet. To be an intercessor is to hold a responsible office. It is equivalent to guard duty outside Buckingham

Palace. No man is always on duty. It is shift work. To be late, absent, or to leave prematurely can have serious consequences. The enemy might choose that very moment to attack. Who will then sound the alarm? Isaiah 62 gives four reasons for continuous intercession by a local church.

Abandoned and forsaken

The church now, as was Jerusalem then, is in a sad state. It is forsaken, abandoned, childless, ruined and a joke to those who see it. I become angry if I overhear someone criticizing, or belittling, my wife when she is dancing. We should be both livid and contrite at the state of the bride—angry at the way it is and yet penitent because we are this body of Christ. It is not somebody's else's fault. We should not smirk if the local church to which we belong is full of growth and life. If some of our brothers and sisters are abandoned and forsaken, we are callous if we are unmoved by their plight. Night and day intercession is the only answer.

Ransacked

The enemy got, and gets, all the good things. It must have been galling to sow seed, to weed and hoe and then have the enemy either destroy or steal the harvest. The best dance, the best music, the best drama, the best art—all these are in the possession of the devil. The church is bankrupt because the devil gets our money. Some churches are more famous for jumble sales than the gospel. We give our time to weeding, washing cars and watching rubbish on the television, rather than to the work of God. We have been ransacked. Continuous intercession is the only solution.

Obstacles

There are boulders on the paths, preventing the restoration of Jerusalem from taking place. The Bishop of Durham, in 1984, was an obstacle to most ordinary people. Many pro-

David Brainerd—eighteenth-century missionary to the Indians of New Jersey and Pennsylvania

The life and diary of David Brainerd by Jonathan Edwards has probably influenced more revivals than any other book. His life was one of burning prayer for the American Indians. He was converted at twenty-one and immediately became a pioneer missionary. He spent six years of astonishing, agonizing prayer until, in 1744, when he was twenty-seven, there came a remarkable revival associated with his work. He died in 1746 aged twenty-nine. Here are two extracts from his 1742 entries when he had been a Christian for three years and was only twenty-four.

In the forenoon, I felt the power of intercession for the advancement of the kingdom of my dear Lord and Saviour in the world; and withal, a most sweet resignation, and even consolation and joy in the thoughts of suffering hardships, distresses, and even death itself, in the promotion of it. In the afternoon God was with me of a truth. Oh, it was a blessed company indeed! My soul was drawn out very much for the world; I think I had more enlargement for sinners, than for the children of God; though I felt as if I could spend my life in cries for both.

I set apart this day for secret fasting and prayer, to entreat God to direct and bless me with regard to the great work I have in view, of preaching the gospel. Just at night the Lord visited me marvellously in prayer: I think my soul never was in such an agony before. I felt no restraint; for the treasures of divine grace were opened to me. I wrestled for absent friends, for the ingathering of souls, and for the children of God in many distant places. I was in such an agony, from sun half an hour high, till near dark, that I was all over wet with sweat; but yet it seemed to me that I had wasted away the day, and had done nothing. Oh, my dear Jesus did sweat blood for poor souls! I longed for more compassion towards them.[8]

testant churches are blinded to the link between their feeble worldly stance on ethical and occult issues (like free-masonry, homosexuality, spiritism, abortion and embryo-experimentation) and the transfer of thinking members from their ranks to the Roman Catholic Church. The humanist thinking and statements of so-called leaders are boulders preventing this restoration. The pathetic ecclesi-astical response to the mass starvation in Ethiopia, com-pared to the Band Aid pop response and the stunning Israeli evacuation, is a boulder. The resurgence of cleri-calism within the house-church movement, and the sus-picion in the historic churches of the doctrine of the priest-hood of all believers, are obstacles. Big events which depend on mass advertising, and big names with inter-national ministries (with photos amongst the adverts of the religious monthlies), both steal the glory from God—truly they have had their reward. The unwillingness of just about everybody to recognize each others' ministries is yet another boulder. The bickering about the position of hands, the wearing of hats, the validity of dance, the use of robes, the gift of tongues, the silence of women—all these argu-ments, and more, prevent the restoration. The pride in buildings, ancient and modern; the acrimony over music, ancient and modern; all of these and many, many more are obstacles which need to be cleared out of the way if the glory of God is to be seen. Intercession is needed. It is needed by night and day.

Marvellous future

Isaiah 62 promises a marvellous future. God will delight in the church. We will be married and, like most brides, we will be given a new name. God has promised that he will hold out his palm and display the church like crown jewels. Our praise will resound around the whole earth! The remembrancers should be continually before God remin-ding him of this, and urging him to bring it about. The link between what the church is and what it will be is found in verses 6 and 7. It is never-ending intercession which will bring about the restoration of Jerusalem. The ancient ruins will be rebuilt on the same foundation. No rest should be taken, and none will be given, until God brings this about.

Clearly no one person can do this on his own. Twenty-four men and twenty-four women maintained the Moravian Chain of Prayer at Herrnhut in the early eighteenth century. That chain of prayer brought about the greatest missionary movement ever seen and the European and American revivals of the 1730s. Throughout history those churches and communities, from the earliest monastic orders to the Ashburnham Stable Family today, which have taken these verses seriously have—through great cost and agony—seen God move in power.

Our own Chain of Prayer is incomplete. This is because of our sin, laziness and disobedience. Yet well over 35,000 hours of intercession have been offered to God in our prayer room during the last seven years. I ask each local church seriously to consider the establishment of a chain of prayer—by night and day—until he come. Already this is beginning to happen. Many churches have experimented with a day or week of unbroken intercession. Others have organized a chain of prayer to coincide with a mission, or time of decision making, or great social need. I think I sense the gentle breeze of the Spirit in this. To attempt organization would destroy this, but let me make a few practical suggestions. Such a chain may be held in the church building or prayer room with the people travelling in to pray. Some traditions find this helpful, others do not. Alternatively, people can pray at their allotted time wherever they are, in the car, home, office, school, laundrette, etc. This is more flexible, but the people feel less part of the chain and this approach is harder to sustain. Some churches have experimented with telephone prayer chains. By this means there are one or two contact numbers which people ring when intercession is urgently required. Each person telephoned has a list of three or four other folk to contact, and in the space of half an hour, several hundred people can be alerted to pray. Perhaps the best home system for a local church is when each member, at the end of their prayer duty, telephones the next one in the rota with the particular needs. This is especially helpful for those praying during the night! The sense of involvement this gives to the elderly will be obvious.

We use a system of prayer cards to guide the intercession, and focus on a few matters and individuals each day. Again, this is easier when a prayer room is used, but such information can be photocopied and distributed by those on duty at the preceding Sunday services. Updates of information can be passed on by the telephone 'baton' change.

We encourage our people to pray in pairs. This is as a result of several prophetic messages which clearly showed that this was God's requirement for us. Some couples pray in the chain for half an hour each month, others pray for up to seven or eight hours at one stretch every week. Some people still pray on their own. I, personally, find that much easier, but try to pray one complete morning each month with a local minister.

Continuous intercession, especially after several years have gone by, is a very strong foundation for ministry and evangelism. I do believe that it is one of the 'wineskins' that God would use in the next few decades, just as prayer meetings have been used in years gone by.

I think that this unceasing intercession should have three distinctive features. Firstly, this intercession should be united. It should be the activity of the whole church, not an enthusiastic core. Secondly, this intercession should be unceasing. It can only happen if everybody takes turns and has clearly delineated duties. Those who find sleep difficult can pray at night. Forty-eight people interceding for half an hour every day can maintain this intercession without growing weary. Finally, this intercession should be 'until...'— until Jerusalem is established, until Christ is vindicated, until he comes to claim his own. It must never stop.

The Role of the Holy Spirit

How can I ever intercede like this? How will I defeat Satan? How will my church pray by night? Whenever we ask the question 'how' the biblical answer is always the same. 'The Holy Spirit. He will come upon you.' Nowhere is this more true than with intercession. The Holy Spirit was promised in Zechariah 12:10 as a spirit of prayer. Jesus, in John 14:16, revealed the Holy Spirit and the potential in prayer as parallel and inseparable. John 14:16 shows the Holy Spirit as the *parakletos* who is just like Jesus. This name suggests that the Holy Spirit is called alongside us, to call from beside us. He is the barrister sent from God, who speaks on our behalf, from our position, to the heavenly Judge. It is the Holy Spirit who lives in our hearts and makes us call out '*Abba*, Father' (Romans 8:15). He enables us to look up at the sky and cry, with a new depth of meaning, 'Our Father'.

Romans 8:26–27 reveals the Spirit's role in intercession. The Holy Spirit intercedes from within us. He helps us in our weakness, especially when we do not know how to pray as we ought. We can do nothing to prevent Christ's intercession for the saints, but we can do everything to prevent or hinder the Spirit's. (Notice whom the Spirit prays for!) He does not intercede, except through us. If we do not intercede, he cannot. He wants our corporate body for his holy temple. He wants all our vocal chords, breath and tongues as the vehicle for his intercession. What a glorious thought it is that when we cry out in prayer it is the Holy Spirit interceding through us.

Ephesians 6:18 and Jude 20 instruct us to pray in the Spirit at all times. The Holy Spirit is both the means of intercession, Ephesians 2:18, and the power for intercession, Romans 8:26–27. He provides us with the energy to overcome our lassitude and get down on our knees. If we are to pray in the Spirit we should recognize and be content with our weakness and ignorance. We must consciously depend on the Spirit to help us in our praying. The man who believes himself to be both strong and knowledgeable will pray in the flesh, not in the Spirit. In 2 Corinthians 12:9–11 Paul boasted of his weaknesses, as he knew that the availability of the power of Christ depended on his weakness. The same principle applies in prayer.

We can ask the Holy Spirit to intercede both through and for us; to act as our advocate. He will either do this in our natural language—in the Spirit, or in an unlearnt language—with the spirit. The mechanism of prayer in the Spirit is the same as for all vocal activity of the Spirit. We provide the physical body and speech-making mechanism. He provides the words. All gifts of the Spirit, all prophesying, all evangelizing, all praying, all worship, follow this same formula. We come in weakness and ignorance and allow the gentle Spirit, or the Spirit of blazing fire, to speak through us. This is not automatic transmission! The Holy Spirit draws from our subconscious all the experiences that are filed away—the songs we have sung, the Collects we have learnt, the books and Bible passages we have read, the verses we have memorized, the prayers we have used or heard others use. At times he may prompt us to use one of these; at other times he will urge us to use our natural thoughts and processes of reasoning to pray extemporarily. On rare occasions the Spirit asks us to pray in our native language, but with no idea as to the succeeding words and sentences. This is not the usual pattern. Normally he provides the thoughts and outline script; the details, vocabulary and syntax are our own contribution.

1 Corinthians 14:15 seems to indicate that our intercession should include both prayer in our own language and prayer in tongues. (Prayer in tongues is dealt with in the Ashburnham Insight book *Tongues and Explanations*.) Prayer in tongues is a pure form of intercession as it is untainted by our human mind. We can be sure that intercession in tongues is exactly according to the mind of God.

Romans 8:26 indicates that prayer in the Spirit will, at times, result in groanings. Some see this as a reference to childbirth. I think it is more plausible that bachelor Paul had Exodus 2:23–25 in his mind. The slaves of Israel groaned to the Lord about their sad plight. They continually reminded God of his covenant promises. He heard their prayer and led them out of Egypt—in his own time and way. Those who know what it means to groan in prayer often die young. Praying Hyde, David Brainerd, Robert Murray M'Cheyne, David Watson, even Jesus of Nazareth, these men all walked the path of prayer, groaning, suffering and glory. Intercession in the Spirit is not the slick and easy recitation of a mantra. It is a costly wrestling, with real groans, but it enables the glory of God to be seen.

Those people and churches who profess to be open to the Spirit should be known by their much praying. We, who are glad to be known as 'charismatics', should be famous for our powerful witness and beautiful worship, but above all things we should be famous for our intercession. If we are not much in prayer, we must be quenching the Spirit.

It is my prayer, and that of all the Ashburnham Stable Family, that you who have read this book will volunteer to live your life out on your knees. We pray that you will take no rest, and remain not silent, until God has restored his church and made her the boast of all the earth. For God's sake, for the sake of his name, his glory, his church and, most of all, his world, please ask him to make you an intercessor.

Let the closing words be given to that remarkable man of prayer who tasted revival—Jonathan Edwards:

> When God has something very great to accomplish for His church it is His will that there should precede it, the extraordinary prayers of His people . . . And it is revealed that when God is about to accomplish great things for His Church, He will begin by remarkably pouring out the spirit of grace and supplication. If we are not to expect that the devil should go out of a particular person, that is under a bodily possession, without extraordinary prayer, or prayer and fasting; how much less should we expect to have him cast out of the land and the world without it.[9]

Notes

1. Charles Finney, 'Meetings for Prayer' Lecture VIII of *Lectures in Revivals of Religion* (Morgan & Scott n.d.).
2. William Law, *A Serious Call to a Devout and Holy Life* (J.M. Dent & Co. 1906), p.277.
3. Andrew Murray, *The Ministry of Intercession* (Lakeland 1972), p.17.
4. William Law, *A Serious Call to a Devout and Holy Life* (J.M. Dent & Co. 1906), p.268.
5. Raymond E. Brown, *The Anchor Bible—The Gospel according to John,* Vol. 29 (Geoffrey Chapman 1971), p.503.
6. D. Martyn Lloyd-Jones, *The Christian Soldier* (The Banner of Truth Trust 1977), p.323.
7. Thomas à Kempis, *The Imitation of Christ* (Penguin 1952), p.100.
8. Jonathan Edwards, *The Life and Diary of David Brainerd* (Moody Press 1980), pp.80, 88.
9. Jonathan Edwards, quoted in Charles Finney, 'Meetings for Prayer' Lecture VIII of *Lectures in Revivals of Religion* (Morgan & Scott n.d.), p.137.